Contents

Words appearing in the text in bold, **like this**, are explained in the Glossary.

Introduction

Our ears are complex organs that allow us to hear a wide variety of different sounds.

- We can detect loud and soft sounds, from the loud roar of a jumbo jet taking off to the quiet purring of a cat.
- We can detect high and low sounds, from the highest note of a piccolo to the lowest bass notes of a church organ.
- We can hear different qualities of sounds, such as the rumble of thunder, the crunching of dry leaves beneath our feet, and the electronic ring of a telephone.
- We can distinguish the tiniest subtle differences in sound, enabling us to know whose voice we are hearing, even when we cannot see the speaker.

All of this information is very important to us, helping us to build up a picture of the world around us.

Our ears also play an important role in allowing us to maintain our balance.

Each ear has three main parts: the outer ear, the **middle ear**, and the **inner ear**.

Outer ear

The **pinna** is the part of the ear that you can see. This flap of skin and **cartilage** at the side of your head acts as a funnel for **sound waves**. It leads to the ear canal, a bony tube inside your head. Stretched across the inner end of the ear canal is a thin **membrane**, called the **eardrum**.

Middle ear

The middle ear is a small space, containing three tiny bones called the **hammer**, the **anvil**, and the **stirrup**. Together, these bones are called **ossicles**. At the end of the middle ear is another membrane, called the **oval window**. A short passage called the **eustachian tube** links the middle ear and the upper part of the throat.

Inner ear

Inside the inner ear, a complicated maze of spaces curls round and round in a bony spiral called the **cochlea**. Signals are transmitted from the cochlea to the brain via the **auditory nerve**. The **semicircular canals**, which control our balance, are also part of the inner ear.

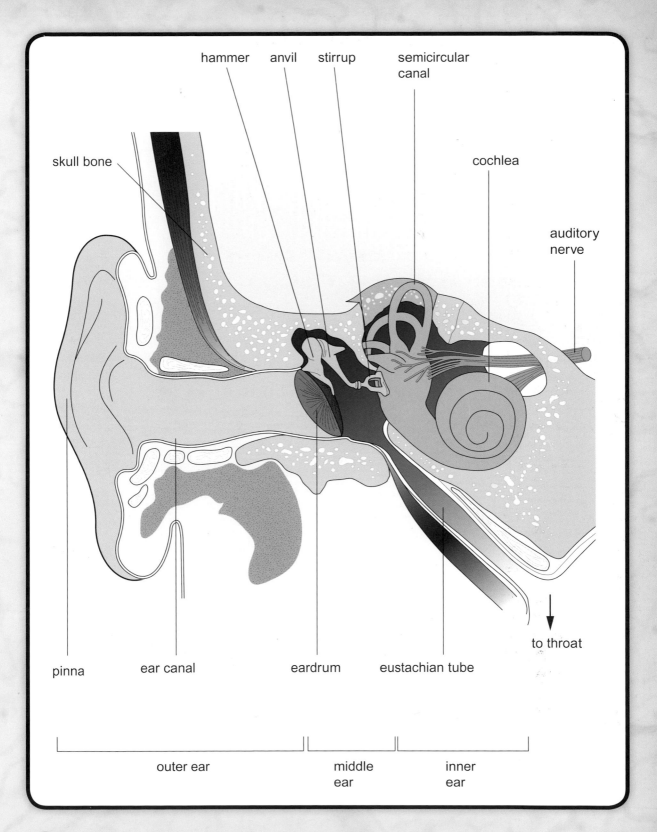

hammer · anvil · stirrup · semicircular canal · cochlea · auditory nerve · skull bone · pinna · ear canal · eardrum · eustachian tube · to throat · outer ear · middle ear · inner ear

This diagram shows the structures of the outer, middle, and inner ear.

Looking after your ears

Your sense of hearing is very important, allowing you to react to sounds and to interact with other people and the world around you. It is important to care for your ears and to avoid damaging them.

Hygiene
Try to keep your ears clean by washing them every day, either with a warm, soapy flannel or under a shower. NEVER put anything in your ear to try to clean it – your ear is very delicate, and you can easily cause irritation or damage.

↑ Pierced ears may look attractive, but it is important to keep them clean so that they do not become infected.

Pierced ears
Many people like to have their ears pierced so that they can wear earrings.

If you decide that you want this done, make sure that you choose a professional to do it. Piercing your own ears, or getting a friend to do it, often causes infection. After piercing, you need to keep your earrings in place until the holes are completely healed. During this time, keep the holes clean and free from infection by washing them with a dilute antiseptic solution once or twice a day. If your ear becomes red, swollen, or painful, tell your parents or doctor straightaway – you may have an infection that will need treatment.

Many schools and sports clubs only allow you to wear small stud earrings. This is for your own safety, because long dangly earrings can get tugged or tangled, which can tear the ear lobe. This is very painful!

HEALTH FOCUS: Swimming
Whenever you swim, your ears are exposed to water that may not be very clean. It is a good idea to rinse your ears with clean water after a swim, and to dry them gently. If your ears feel blocked, or you cannot hear properly after swimming, some water may be trapped in the ear canal. This is nothing to worry about, and the water will usually just drain away on its own.

Loud noises

Loud noises can damage the delicate structures of the ear and lead to deafness. We cannot protect our ears from all the loud noises around us, but it makes sense to reduce those that we can.

MP3 players and headphones can easily be turned up to levels that may seriously damage the ears. Read the instructions that come with your equipment and try to keep the volume low – if other people can hear, it is too loud for your ears.

There is a risk of permanent hearing loss from listening to music at 89 decibels (dB) for more than an hour a day over a five-year period. Many MP3 players have a maximum volume of 100 dB.

Prolonged exposure to loud music at concerts and clubs can also lead to deafness. Some rock stars who have played very loud music for many years suffer from serious hearing loss. You can protect your ears by wearing earplugs – they won't stop you hearing and enjoying the music, but they will reduce the likelihood of damaging your ears.

Keeping the volume low on your MP3 player can help to avoid damaging your ears.

HEALTH FOCUS: Ear protection

Ears can be protected from machinery noise or other loud sounds by wearing earmuffs or earplugs. It makes sense to wear these whenever you are in noisy conditions, because loud noises can cause ear damage.

Outer ear

The outer ear is made up of the **pinna**, the external auditory canal, and the **eardrum**.

Pinna

The part of your ear that you can see at the side of your head is called the pinna. It is a flap of bendy **cartilage** covered with skin, and is attached to the head with **ligaments** and muscles. Although different people have pinnae of different shapes and sizes, they all have the same basic structure. The curves of the pinna act as a funnel, collecting **sound waves** and channelling them into the ear canal.

Many animals are able to move their pinnae. Some can swivel them around to the direction of a sound to increase their level of hearing; others use them to waft air around, to help them stay cool. Humans have lost the ability to move their pinnae, although some people can control the tiny muscles that allow them to waggle just the tip of their ear lobe.

Ear lobes come in one of two basic shapes: either as a gentle curve away from the side of the head (attached lobe), or with a dip down and up again (free lobe). These shapes tend to run in families, and are inherited in a similar way to eye and hair colour.

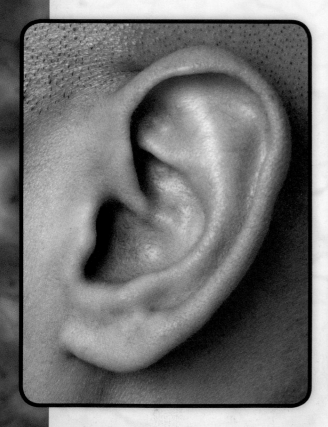

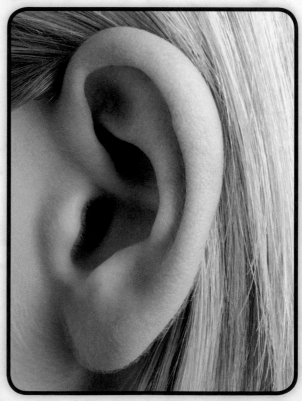

 These two photographs show two common ear lobe shapes: an attached lobe on the left and a free lobe on the right. Have a look in a mirror at your own lobe shape, and then check out the rest of your family.

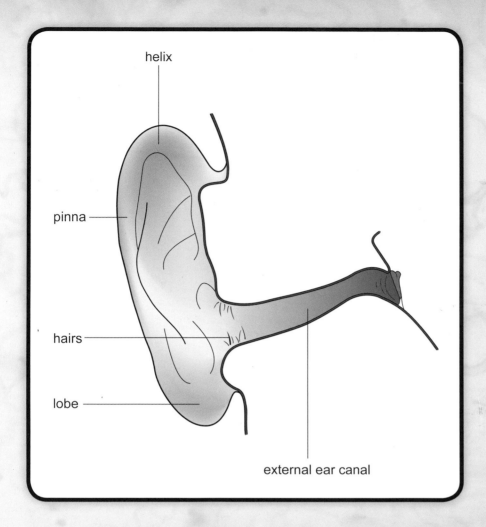

helix

pinna

hairs

lobe

external ear canal

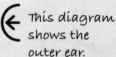
This diagram shows the outer ear.

External ear canal

This narrow tube is 2–3 centimetres (1–1½ inches) long, stretching from the pinna to the eardrum. The outer third of the ear canal is made of flexible cartilage, and the rest is channelled out of the bones of the skull. The external ear canal helps to protect the eardrum from changes in temperature and humidity.

The cartilage and bone of the ear canal are covered with skin. Fine hairs grow from the skin, pointing outwards towards the pinna. Ceruminous glands in the skin produce cerumen (earwax). This helps to keep the skin of the ear canal moist. It also traps dead skin, dust particles, and microbes, and together with the hairs, it helps to prevent dirt reaching the eardrum. Earwax usually dries up and falls out of the ear canal naturally.

Outer ear problems

Getting stuck!

The golden rule is never to put anything into your ear – it is amazingly easy for things to get stuck in there! Very young children playing with small toys sometimes put them in their ears – they may just be finding out about their bodies, or be playing and not realize the danger of what they are doing. Often, the help of a doctor is needed to remove the object. Adults cleaning their ears with cotton wool buds or twists of tissue may also end up with a piece stuck in the ear canal and find that they, too, cannot remove it without help.

Too much wax

Earwax usually dries up and is pushed outwards along the ear canal by tiny hairs, eventually falling out on its own. Some people, especially those with very dusty jobs, produce a lot of earwax. It may build up in the ear canal, causing irritation, noises in the ear, and dulled hearing. Attempts to remove it with cotton wool buds or hairpins often only push it in even further. A doctor can easily remove excess wax by softening it (for example, with a few drops of warm olive oil), and then using a jet of warm water and a syringe to suck the wax out. The ear can then be cleaned and dried, and hearing should be normal again. It may not sound pleasant, but syringing the ears like this should not hurt at all.

↑ Medical staff may syringe a patient's ears to remove excess earwax.

HEALTH FOCUS: Infections

The outer ear can become infected by **bacteria**. If this happens, a sticky liquid may ooze from the ear. The person may also be slightly deaf in the infected ear if the liquid blocks the ear canal.

Infections can easily be treated with **antibiotics**, either as tablets or as eardrops. As the infection clears, the person's hearing will return to normal.

Cauliflower ears

Some sports can cause frequent **abrasion** and rubbing of the **pinna**, resulting in the damage that we call "cauliflower ear". Many players protect their ears with a full helmet, or a scrum cap such as those used in rugby. Others may tape their ears flat to the head to avoid damage. If you play a sport where your ears may be damaged, it is important to do all you can to protect them.

This rugby player's ears are badly damaged after years of abrasion and rubbing. The lumpy appearance is typical of "cauliflower ear". Many players wear protective headgear to prevent this type of damage.

Middle ear

As its name suggests, the **middle ear** lies between the outer ear and the **inner ear**. It is a small space within the skull bones and contains the **ossicles**, the smallest bones in the human body.

The middle ear is a narrow, irregular shape that is filled with air. It is separated from the ear canal by the **eardrum**. Two further **membranes**, the **oval window** and the **round window**, separate the middle ear from the inner ear.

Eustachian tube

The **eustachian tube** (also called the auditory tube) forms a link between the middle ear and the back of the upper mouth (the nasopharynx, a space between the nasal passages and the soft palate). The main purpose of the eustachian tube is to keep the air pressure inside the middle ear the same as the air pressure in the ear canal. If the difference in pressures is too great, the eardrum may be distorted. The eustachian tube maintains the balance of pressures by allowing air from the nasal cavity to pass into the middle ear. The eustachian tube stays closed while the pressures are balanced; if the outside pressure is greater than the inside pressure, the eustachian tube opens, allowing air to flow from the nose into the middle ear. You have probably felt your ears "pop" as the pressure inside adjusts at some time, perhaps in a car going uphill or on a fairground ride.

 This diagram shows the structures inside the middle ear.

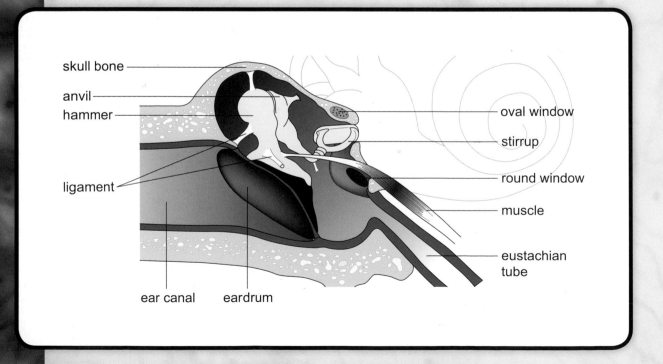

skull bone

anvil

hammer

oval window

stirrup

round window

ligament

muscle

eustachian tube

ear canal   eardrum

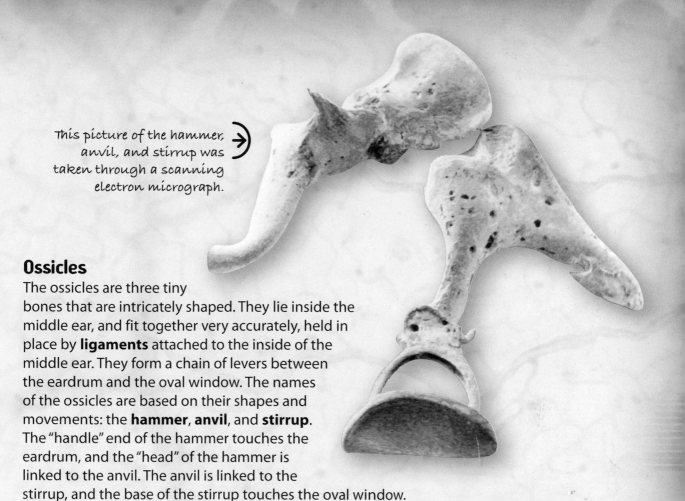

This picture of the hammer, anvil, and stirrup was taken through a scanning electron micrograph.

Ossicles

The ossicles are three tiny bones that are intricately shaped. They lie inside the middle ear, and fit together very accurately, held in place by **ligaments** attached to the inside of the middle ear. They form a chain of levers between the eardrum and the oval window. The names of the ossicles are based on their shapes and movements: the **hammer**, **anvil**, and **stirrup**. The "handle" end of the hammer touches the eardrum, and the "head" of the hammer is linked to the anvil. The anvil is linked to the stirrup, and the base of the stirrup touches the oval window.

Two tiny, delicate muscles control the movements of the ossicles. One is attached to the head of the hammer, and limits the size of its movements, protecting the middle ear from very loud noises. The other is attached to the neck of the stirrup, and limits its movement. This protects the oval window, but makes our hearing less sensitive.

Loud noises

Although the muscles respond very quickly when there is a sudden loud sound, they cannot contract instantly. They can protect our ears from continuous loud noises, such as machinery, but they cannot respond quickly enough to protect the ears from very sudden, short noises, such as a gunshot.

HEALTH FOCUS: Pressure changes

The eustachian tube may not open quickly enough if there are sudden pressure changes, such as when taking off or landing in an aeroplane. It opens naturally when we yawn and swallow, so we can often relieve any discomfort by doing this. Sucking a boiled sweet can help reduce the problem as it encourages a swallowing action.

Middle ear problems

Otitis media

Otitis media is the medical term for a **middle ear** infection. It usually follows a sore throat or a cold, when **viruses** and **bacteria** may travel to the middle ear via the **eustachian tube**. The middle ear becomes inflamed and extremely painful. Pus is produced and, because it cannot drain away, the pressure inside the middle ear increases. Ringing noises and other sounds may be heard inside the ear, and hearing is reduced. The **eardrum** becomes red and bulges outwards. In severe cases, the eardrum may even burst, allowing pus to drain out of the ear canal. Usually the infection is treated with **antibiotics**, preventing it reaching this level of severity. When the infection is cleared up, hearing returns to normal.

This photograph is of a culture of *Alloiococcus otitidis*, a bacterium that is responsible for many middle ear infections.

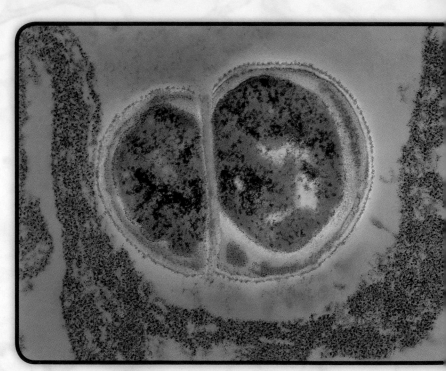

Glue ear

Glue ear affects one in ten children at some time during their childhood. It is a form of otitis media and is the result of chronic inflammation of the middle ear, possibly caused by persistent infections or allergies. The eustachian tube does not work properly, so air cannot reach the middle ear. Thick fluid builds up inside the middle ear, and stops the **ossicles** moving freely, so that the child gradually loses hearing. Treatment is usually with decongestant medicine. In some cases, however, a minor operation is necessary. Fluid can be drained away by making a tiny hole in the eardrum. A small plastic tube called a grommet is put into the hole, allowing air to reach the middle ear. The ear can then slowly return to normal. As the eardrum grows, the grommet is slowly pushed out.

Although glue ear is not dangerous and does not cause long-term hearing loss, it is important to detect it as soon as possible. Hearing plays a vital role in the learning process, and if a child's hearing is reduced for a while their education is likely to suffer.

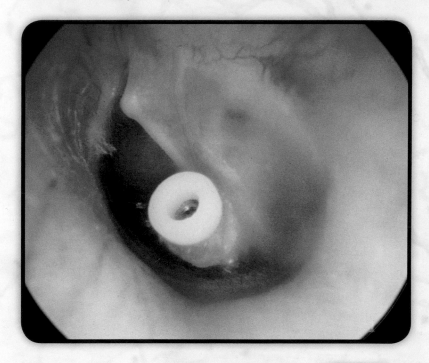

A grommet like this may be inserted into a hole in the eardrum if a child is suffering from glue ear.

Otosclerosis

Otosclerosis is quite a rare condition, noticed usually in teenagers and young adults. It affects more women than men, and scientists think that there may be a **genetic** cause, because it tends to run in families. The ability of the ossicles to transmit vibrations gradually decreases as extra bone material is produced around the **stirrup**. The ossicles become stiff, and hearing is slowly reduced, resulting eventually in deafness.

Several types of treatment are available. The faulty stirrup may be removed, and a plastic one inserted in its place. Surgery may be carried out to reduce the amount of extra bone around the stirrup, restoring its freedom of movement. Hearing aids have been developed to bypass the ossicles – they transmit **sound waves** to the **inner ear** via the skull bones.

HEALTH FOCUS: Cholesteatoma

Cholesteatoma is a rare but serious condition in which a cyst develops inside the middle ear, causing pain, fluid discharge, and hearing loss. As the cyst grows, it destroys the surrounding bone and may also destroy the eardrum and the bones of the middle ear. The cyst can be removed by surgery, but it may take several operations to remove it entirely.

Inner ear

The **inner ear** lies within the bones of the skull, protected from injury and damage. Unlike the outer ear and **middle ear**, the inner ear is filled with fluid. It contains the final part of the chain of structures that allow us to hear, and the sensitive organs that are concerned with balance. The inner ear is also called the "labyrinth", because its complicated spiral structure of canals is rather like a maze.

The bones of the skull are hollowed out, creating a bony space lined with a thin **membrane**. The central area of this space is called the vestibule, and is separated from the middle ear by the **oval window**.

There are two main parts of the inner ear:
- the organs concerned with balance: the **semicircular canals**, **utricle**, and **saccule** (see pages 22–23)
- the spiral **cochlea**, which is concerned with hearing.

The semicircular canals are sensitive to rotational movements of the head. There are three semicircular canals, two vertical and one horizontal, arranged at right angles to each other, like three sides of a cube. Each detects tiny movements of the head in one direction and sends signals to the brain, providing information about the speed and direction of movement.

The utricle and saccule are sensitive to changes of posture. They send signals to the brain, providing information when the head tilts from side to side or tips backwards and forwards.

Together, these structures allow the brain to pinpoint precisely the movements and position of the head.

 This diagram shows the structures of the inner ear.

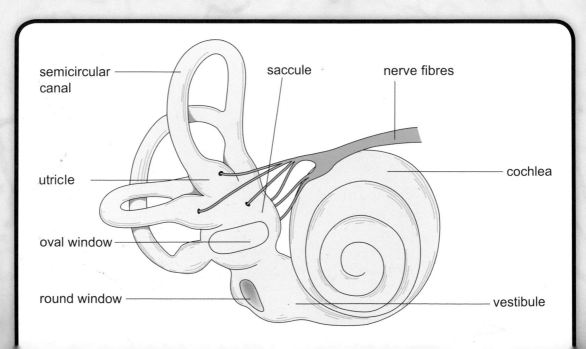

semicircular canal

saccule

nerve fibres

utricle

cochlea

oval window

round window

vestibule

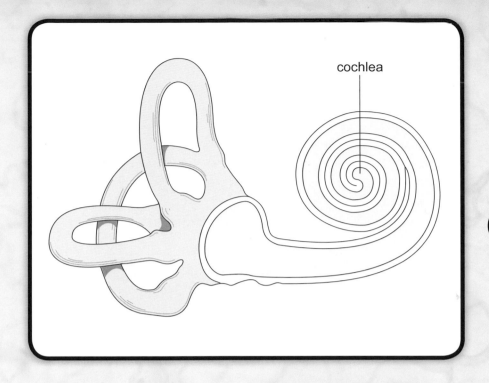

cochlea

The cochlea spirals round two and three-quarter times.

Cochlea

The cochlea gets its name from the Greek word for a snail, "*kokhlos*", because it spirals round like a snail's shell. It is a bony tube that winds round on itself two and three-quarter times. There is a central bony core, with three ducts running in parallel along its length, just as wires run together along a length of electrical cable. Each duct is separated from the others by a membrane.

The central duct contains the **spiral organ**, and it is this that allows us to hear sounds. It has a complicated arrangement of **hair cells**, each with bristle-like sensory hairs. Each hair cell is linked to nerve fibres, and these join larger bundles of nerves to carry signals from the cochlea to the auditory area of the brain.

The base of the cochlea is separated from the middle ear by another membrane, which covers a bony hole called the **round window**.

IN FOCUS: DISCOVERY OF THE COCHLEA

In 1561, an Italian professor called Gabriello Fallopio discovered the cochlea, although he mistakenly thought that it was filled with air. It was nearly 300 years later, in 1851, that improved microscopes allowed another Italian scientist, Alfonso Corti, to examine the structure of the inner ear more closely. He discovered that the cochlea was filled with liquid, and was even able to see the tiny hair cells. For many years, the spiral organ was known as the "Organ of Corti".

Inner ear problems

Inner ear problems can be the result of the **cochlea** not functioning properly, or a failure of the **auditory nerve** to carry signals to the brain. These problems can be caused by a reduction in the blood supply to the ears, due to narrowing of the arteries, exposure to loud noises, or head injuries. They can also be caused by some drugs and by some diseases, including mumps and meningitis. If a pregnant woman catches rubella (German measles), it can cause serious damage to her baby's ears.

Ménières disease

Ménières disease is caused by excess fluid in the inner ear, which increases the pressure inside. A patient usually has a bad attack of vertigo (dizziness) and a feeling of sickness, together with a loss of hearing. The ears may feel full and about to burst, accompanied by roaring and hissing sounds. Attacks may last just a few minutes or for several hours. After each attack, everything slowly returns to normal although, over a period of time, the person's hearing gradually deteriorates. Some drugs can help to reduce the symptoms and, in some cases, an operation to drain away the excess fluid can help. In other patients, special hearing aids can help, but may not solve the problem completely.

 Many people use hearing aids, such as this one, to help them hear more clearly.

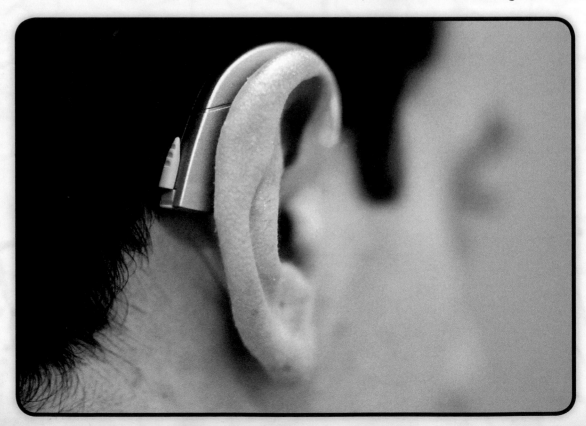

HEALTH FOCUS: Labyrinthitis

Labyrinthitis is inflammation of the inner ear, usually caused by a **bacterial** or **viral** infection, allergies, or toxic drugs. The person feels dizzy and sick, and loses their sense of hearing. They often fall over, in the direction of the affected ear. Labyrinthitis can usually be treated successfully with drugs, with no permanent hearing loss.

Tinnitus

Tinnitus is the name given to hearing ringing or buzzing noises that do not actually exist. It is not really one single problem, but can be the result of several different problems. It can be caused by outer ear problems, such as earwax stuck in the ear canal, and by **middle ear** problems, such as infections. Most commonly, though, it arises as a result of damage to the cochlea. Although some drugs may help a little, tinnitus is difficult to treat. Some patients wear a "masking device", a small piece of equipment that fits into the ear like a hearing aid. This produces a constant noise that takes the patient's attention away from the irritating tinnitus sounds.

Presbyacusis

As people age, their sense of hearing slowly deteriorates, because **hair cells** in the cochlea are gradually lost. This process is called presbyacusis. The ability to hear high **frequency** sounds is usually lost before the ability to hear low frequency sounds. Elderly people can often hear a mumbling noise when people speak to them, but are unable to distinguish words clearly. Hearing aids can often be used to amplify the frequencies that a person cannot detect, allowing them to hear more clearly again.

Beethoven suffered from the ringing and roaring sounds of tinnitus for many years.

Balance: which way is up?

The **inner ear** plays an important part in helping you to keep your balance. The **utricle** and **saccule** both help your body to know instinctively which way is up. They are also involved in the detection of sudden head movements.

The walls of the utricle and saccule each contain a small area that is thicker than the rest. These are called the maculae (one is a macula), and they are perpendicular to each other. They contain the receptors that collect information about the position of the head, allowing us to keep our bodies balanced.

Each macula contains **hair cells** and supporting cells. Each hair cell is linked to nerve fibres. A jelly-like layer, called the **otolithic membrane**, lies on top of the hair cells. The surface of this membrane is covered by a layer of calcium carbonate granules, called **otoliths**.

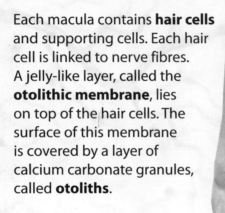

Gymnasts rely on their sense of balance for many of their intricate moves.

IN FOCUS: SOMERSAULT!

We spend most of our waking life with our heads pointing upwards. In some sports, though, people turn upside down rapidly over and over again. The hair cells in the maculae are bent backwards and forwards quickly when gymnasts and divers turn one somersault after another!

Forwards and backwards

When you tilt your head forwards, the otolithic membrane and the otoliths are pulled by gravity. This makes them slide over the hair cells. As they slide, they bend the hair cells, and the hair cells respond by sending signals to the brain. When the brain receives the signal, it interprets the information about the direction in which the head is tilted.

When you tilt your head backwards, the otolithic membrane and otoliths are pulled in the opposite direction, and the hair cells are bent in the opposite direction.

Because it depends just on gravity, and does not rely on any visual information, this system should work without any visual signals. Most of the time it does – for example, when you are underwater or in complete darkness, you can still tell which way is up. The system can get confused, though – it is not unknown for an aeroplane pilot to be flying upside down in dense cloud and not realize!

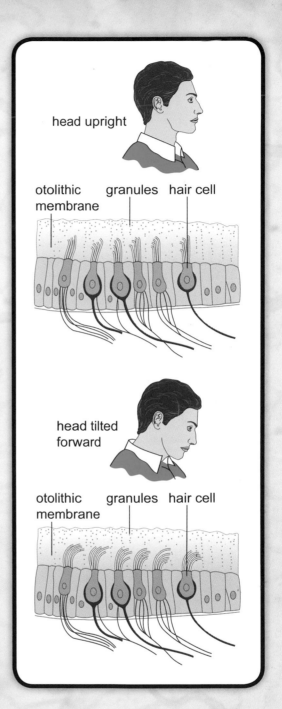

These diagrams show how the hair cells in the macula are bent when the head is tilted forwards.

IN FOCUS: IN SPACE

Astronauts find it difficult to tell which way is up. The utricle and saccule rely on the pull of gravity to move the otolithic membrane and otoliths. In the zero gravity of space, there is no pull, and so this mechanism does not work.

Balance: moving around

Whether we are moving or still, we need to maintain our balance. Movements of the head are detected by the **semicircular canals** in the **inner ear**, and this information is passed to the brain for processing and action.

The inner ear contains three semicircular canals set at right angles to each other, like three sides of a cube. They respond to turning and rotating movements of the head.

Semicircular canal

Each semicircular canal is filled with fluid. In each is a bulge, called an ampulla. Inside each ampulla is a raised area, called the crista, with a patch of **hair cells** and supporting cells. The hair cells stick out into a jelly-like flap called a cupula. The mechanism works rather like a hinged door: the crista is the doorframe and hinge; the cupula is free to swing to and fro, like a door opening and closing.

As the cupula moves, its free edge brushes against the curved wall of the ampulla. When the head rotates, the fluid in the semicircular canal lags behind, pushing the cupula and bending the hair cells. As they bend, the hair cells send signals to the brain. It receives the signals and interprets the information about the direction in which the head is moving.

The semicircular canals can only detect quick, jerky movements. They cannot detect slow, steady movements, because then the fluid inside them does not lag behind.

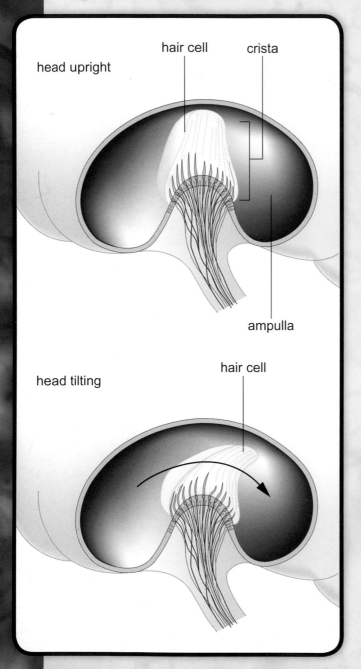

head upright

hair cell   crista

ampulla

head tilting

hair cell

 These diagrams show how the hair cells of the semicircular canals are bent when the head rotates.

Feeling dizzy

If you spin round and round quickly, you often feel dizzy when you stop. This is because the fluid in the semicircular canals keeps moving for a short while, even when your head is still, so it continues to bend the hair cells. You know you are not moving, but your brain Is still receiving signals from the inner ear telling it that you are moving. You feel dizzy – you may feel you are still moving, but in the opposite direction to that in which you were spinning, or you may feel that you are still, and that everything around you is moving.

The inner ear of those people who are deaf and dumb often does not function at all, so they never feel dizzy!

The semicircular canals do not rely on the pull of gravity, so they do work in zero gravity. Astronauts have no problems with detecting their head movements.

Ice-skaters fix their eyes on one spot to avoid feeling dizzy when they stop spinning.

HEALTH FOCUS: Dizziness

The feeling of dizziness can be a problem for people who spin around a lot, such as ice-skaters and ballet dancers. To pirouette, they train themselves to keep their eyes fixed on one spot, so that with each spin their eyes go back to that spot. This helps them to avoid feeling dizzy when they stop.

Motion sickness

Most people have experienced motion sickness at some time. You may feel sick travelling in a car, bus, or boat. We get this sensation when the messages sent to the brain from our eyes and ears contradict each other. There are also other factors that may be involved.

Symptoms

Some people suffer from motion sickness however they travel, while others may only suffer in one particular type of transport. Motion sickness usually causes a person to look pale and feel sick. Many people suffer a cold sweat and are actually sick.

Motion sickness arises when the brain receives conflicting signals from the eyes and **inner ears**. For example, if you are a passenger in a car, your inner ears detect no movement because the forward movement of the car is steady, but your eyes detect the movement of the scenery passing by. The brain receives signals from the ears telling it you are not moving, but signals from the eyes tell it you are moving. Putting these two together can cause a problem – and you sometimes feel sick.

The opposite happens if you are in a windowless room within a boat. Your ears detect the rocking movement of the boat, but your eyes detect no movement in your surroundings. Again, the brain receives conflicting signals and you can feel sick.

 Fairground rides that spin you round can make you feel dizzy and sick.

Reading in a car can increase a feeling of motion sickness. Looking forwards out of the windscreen can help to relieve the problem.

Other factors are involved in motion sickness. If you have had motion sickness before, you may unconsciously expect to be sick again, and this expectation can make you feel sick. Psychologists call this a "conditioned reflex".

How to avoid it

To avoid motion sickness, you need to try to match the two sets of signals as much as you can. In a car, looking forwards out of the windscreen will minimize the visual movement. In a boat, looking at the horizon will balance the actual movement and the visual movement.

Children between the ages of 4 and 12 are most likely to suffer from motion sickness, although many children never experience this problem at all. Many people slowly adjust and, by the time they are teenagers, they know what they should avoid – for example, reading in a car can make many people feel sick. However, some people are not able to adjust, and may suffer from motion sickness all their lives.

HEALTH FOCUS: Remedies for motion sickness

Drugs are available to help combat motion sickness. Some work by suppressing the balance system, and others work by suppressing vomiting. These can cause drowsiness, and many people prefer to rely on drug-free remedies. These include stretchy wristbands that press on acupuncture points, and herbal remedies, such as eating ginger. Avoiding heavy meals, especially fatty, fried foods, can help to reduce the feelings of sickness. Fresh air is important, too, because a stuffy atmosphere can lead to sleepiness and sickness.

How do we hear?

When a sound is made, vibrations spread out in all directions from the source of the sound. These vibrations, called **sound waves**, travel through the air. We hear the sound when these vibrations enter our ears.

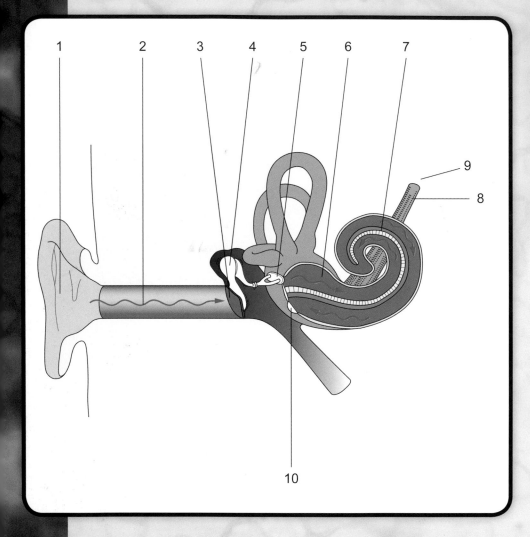

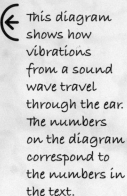

This diagram shows how vibrations from a sound wave travel through the ear. The numbers on the diagram correspond to the numbers in the text.

The outer ear, **middle ear**, and **inner ear** all play a part in allowing us to hear sounds. When a sound wave enters our ear, a rapid sequence of events begins that results in our "hearing" the sound.

1. The **pinna** acts as a funnel, channelling sound waves into the ear canal.
2. Sound waves travel inwards along the ear canal.
3. When the sound waves reach the **eardrum**, they make it vibrate.
4. As the eardrum vibrates backwards and forwards, it makes the **hammer** vibrate. This makes the **anvil** vibrate, which, in turn, makes the **stirrup** vibrate.
5. The vibrations of the stirrup make the **oval window** vibrate.
6. The vibrations of the oval window cause the fluid in the **cochlea** to vibrate.
7. As the fluid vibrates, it bends some of the **hair cells** of the cochlea.

8. The hair cells that are bent send electrical signals to the brain via the **auditory nerve**.
9. The brain receives the signals and interprets the information. You "hear" the sound.
10. Pressure waves travel to the **round window**, making it bulge outwards. The waves are lost as the pressure passes into the middle ear and is equalised by the **eustachian tube**.

IN FOCUS: DIFFERENT EARS

Mammals' ears may be different shapes, but they all have the same basic structure. Other animals have very different ears. Some creatures have no outer ear, but have their eardrum on the surface of the body, with a simplified internal system. This arrangement is called a tympanal organ. In frogs, the tympanal organs are on the side of the head. In other creatures, such as crickets, they are on their legs.

Sound waves travel through the air away from the sound source, just as these ripples travel away from a stone dropped into a pond.

Cochlea

The **cochlea** is the coiled structure within the **inner ear** that responds to the vibrations of the **sound waves** by transmitting electrical signals to the brain.

As the diagram on page 17 shows, the cochlea is a bony spiral. Inside the central duct of this spiral is the **spiral organ**. This is a coiled sheet of cells, including **hair cells** and supporting cells. The hair cells are connected to nerve cells.

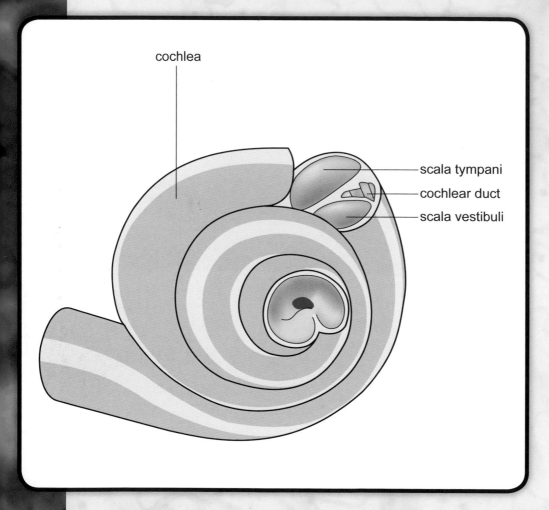

cochlea

scala tympani

cochlear duct

scala vestibuli

In this diagram, you can see the structure of the bony spiral of the cochlea.

Hair cells

There are two groups of hair cells: the inner hair cells and the outer hair cells. Inner hair cells are arranged in a single row that extends along the whole length of the cochlea. More than 90 per cent of these cells are connected to nerve cells that carry information to the brain.

Outer hair cells are arranged in three rows. Most of these cells are also connected to nerve cells. On each hair cell, the hairs are arranged in the pattern of a "U" or a "W". The tips of each hair cell are embedded in a jelly-like layer, the **tectorial membrane**.

How does the cochlea work?

When a sound wave reaches the outer ear, it is transmitted through the **middle ear**, and eventually the vibrations reach the inner ear. Pressure waves are created in the fluid in the cochlea, and these waves make the **basilar membrane** vibrate. This makes the hair cells move. As they move, they brush against the tectorial membrane and their tips are bent. They respond to this bending by sending signals along the nerve cells to which they are connected.

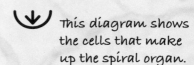

This diagram shows the cells that make up the spiral organ.

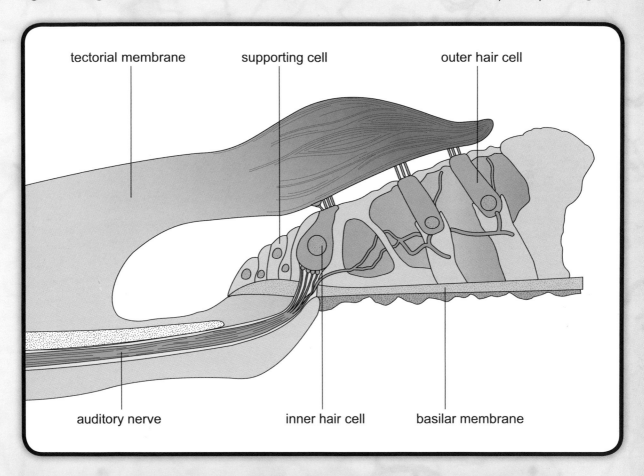

tectorial membrane supporting cell outer hair cell

auditory nerve inner hair cell basilar membrane

IN FOCUS: MAKING SOUNDS

Amazingly, the cochlea itself can also produce sounds! As the outer hair cells move, they cause vibrations that can be detected by a doctor using a very sensitive microphone placed next to the **eardrum**. These sounds can be useful in the detection of hearing defects in newborn babies: if no sounds are produced, it shows that the outer hair cells are not moving and the cochlea is not responding to vibrations.

Cochlear implants

Cochlear implants can be used to restore some hearing in people whose own **cochleas** are not functioning. These small electronic devices bypass the cochlea and send tiny electrical signals directly to the brain.

What is a cochlear implant?

Cochlear implants are usually made up of five parts: a small microphone worn behind the ear; a sound processor that may be carried in a pocket; a transmitting coil behind the ear; a receiver/stimulator implanted behind the ear; and an electrode array implanted into the cochlea.

The technology involved in cochlear implant devices is continually advancing. Devices are likely to get smaller and work more efficiently as designs become increasingly sophisticated.

Cochlear implants do not yet provide a normal standard of hearing, but most people with implants are able to hear medium and loud sounds. Some are able to hear well enough to be able to use the telephone, which they would be unable to do without the implant.

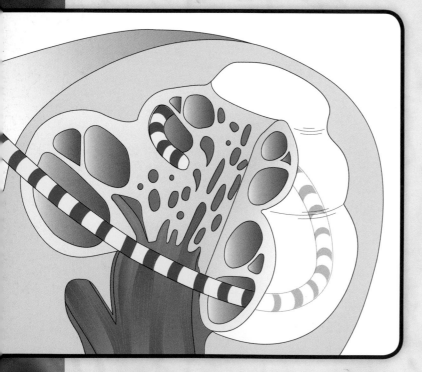

This diagram shows how the electrode array (shown here as the red and yellow striped tube) coils round inside the cochlea.

How does an implant work?

1. The microphone detects a sound and sends it to the sound processor.
2. The sound processor amplifies and filters the sound, and turns it into electrical signals that it sends to the transmitting coil.
3. The transmitting coil passes the signals to the receiver/stimulator.
4. The receiver/stimulator stimulates electrodes in the electrode array.
5. The electrodes stimulate the **auditory nerve**.
6. The auditory nerve transmits the signals to the auditory centre in the brain, as in normal hearing.
7. The person "hears" the sound.

How does a patient receive an implant?

Cochlear implants are placed using surgery. The operation usually takes a couple of hours. A small cut is made in the skin just behind the ear, and the receiver/stimulator is placed against the skull bone. A tiny hole is drilled in the skull bone, allowing an even tinier hole to be drilled in the cochlea. The electrode array is then gently inserted into the cochlea through this hole. The wound is stitched, and given time to heal. After a few weeks, the other parts of the implant can be fitted, and **audiologists** make sure that the sound level is comfortable for the person. Regular check-ups are necessary to ensure that the settings are right, and that the implant is working properly.

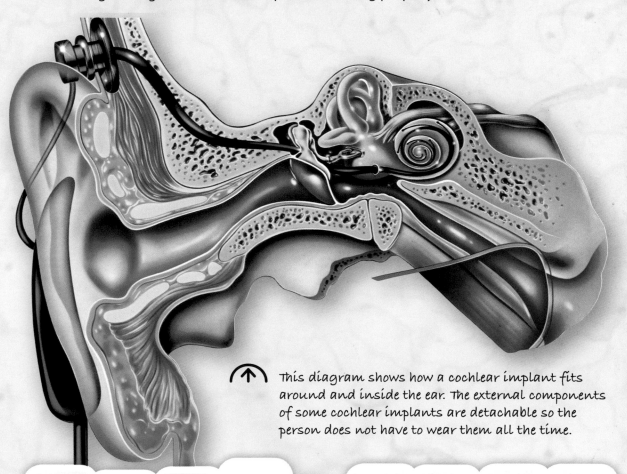

This diagram shows how a cochlear implant fits around and inside the ear. The external components of some cochlear implants are detachable so the person does not have to wear them all the time.

HEALTH FOCUS: Living with a cochlear implant

It can take a while to get used to hearing again. People who have been deaf for a long time may need support and help to enable them to communicate effectively. Children who have never heard any sound at all can react in a variety of ways – some are happy, others can be puzzled. Also, not everyone agrees with the use of the implant. Many people do not see their deafness as a disability, and are not in favour of seeing deafness surgically altered.

Different sounds

The human ear can detect a wide variety of differences between sounds, such as whether they are high or low, loud or soft. We can also detect differences in the quality of a sound and can often tell what has made the sound – for example, we can tell whether a sound is made by metal hitting metal or wood hitting wood.

High and low

The **pitch** is the term we give to how high or low a sound is. The pitch of a sound depends on the speed of the vibrations: the faster the vibrations, the higher the pitch. The speed of the vibrations is called the **frequency** and is measured in Hertz (Hz): 1 Hz = 1 cycle per second. Human ears can usually hear sounds that vibrate between 20 and 20,000 cycles every second (20 Hz–20,000 Hz). Human speech usually contains sounds between 100 and 3,000 Hz. Some animals, such as dogs and bats, can hear very high frequency sounds that are inaudible to human ears.

Detecting pitch

We can detect differences in pitch because each part of the **cochlea** responds to a different frequency of vibration. High-pitched sounds, with fast vibrations, are detected by the part of the cochlea closest to the **oval window**. Low-pitched sounds, with slow vibrations, are detected by the other end of the cochlea. When the brain receives the signal via the **auditory nerve**, it knows which part of the cochlea has responded to the sound and, therefore, it knows what the pitch of the sound must be.

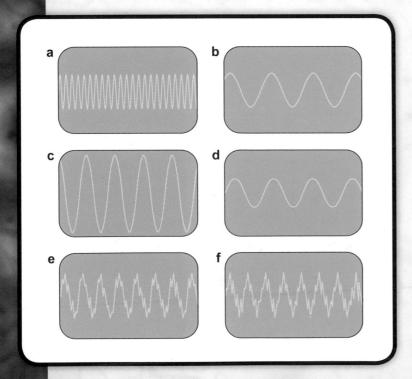

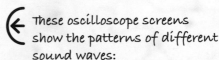
These oscilloscope screens show the patterns of different sound waves:

a) very fast vibrations – high-pitched sound
b) very slow vibrations – low-pitched sound
c) very big vibrations – loud sound
d) very small vibrations – soft sound
e) a recorder playing middle C
f) a woman singing middle C.

In (e) and (f), the notes have the same pitch and volume, but the wave patterns are different because the mixtures of noises are different.

Loud and soft

The loudness of a sound as it reaches your **eardrum** is called the volume. The intensity of a sound is the amount of energy in the **sound waves**. If you are a long way from a high-intensity sound, its volume may be less than that of a low-intensity sound that is close to you. Intensity is measured in decibels (dB). The quietest sound that can be detected by a normal human ear is given a value of 0 dB, and is called the "threshold of hearing". The table below shows the intensity of some everyday sounds.

sound	intensity
whispering	30 dB
normal conversation	60 dB
shouting/screaming	80 dB
thunder	100 dB
aeroplane taking off	120 dB

We can detect differences in the volume of sounds because of differences in the sizes of the vibrations: the louder the sound, the bigger the vibration. Bigger vibrations stimulate more **hair cells**, so that more signals are sent to the brain. The brain interprets the information, knowing that the more signals it receives, the louder the sound must be.

IN FOCUS: THE QUALITY OF SOUND

Few sounds are pure — most are made up of a mixture of noises. You can compare sound to colour: only red, blue, and yellow are primary colours, but these three can be mixed together in different proportions to produce all the colours of the rainbow. Sounds are similar — each is made of a distinctive mixture of high and low, loud and soft components, mixed together to form a huge range of sounds. The brain recognizes each specific mixture it receives via the cochlea and identifies the sound.

Sounds all around

When we hear a sound, we can often tell which direction it came from. This is because we have two ears, positioned on opposite sides of our heads, each of which receives a slightly different sound and passes a slightly different signal to the brain.

Sound waves

When a sound is made, **sound waves** travel through the air. Unless the sound source is directly in front, behind, or above you, one ear will be closer to the sound source than the other. The sound waves will reach the nearer ear before they reach the other ear. For this reason, signals from the nearer ear reach the brain before signals from the other ear. This difference is tiny – about 1/1,500 of a second! The brain can detect the difference, and can use the information to pinpoint the direction of the sound.

As the sound waves travel away from the sound source, the vibrations gradually get smaller, just as ripples in a pond get smaller as they spread out from a stone dropped into the water. This means that the further away from the sound source you are, the quieter the sound will be. The ear that is nearer to the sound source will receive very slightly bigger vibrations than the other ear. More **hair cells** will be stimulated in the nearer ear than in the other ear. The brain can detect this difference, and this information helps it to pinpoint the direction of the sound.

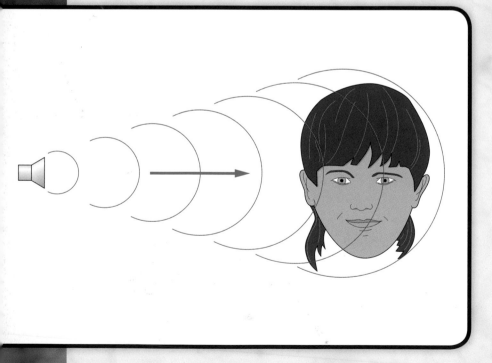

The ear that is nearer to the sound source receives the vibration a fraction of a second before the other ear. It also hears a slightly louder sound than the other ear.

Moving ears

Most mammals can move their ear **pinnae** to help them to locate the direction of a sound. Humans cannot do this – instead, we must move our heads.

Locating sounds relies on signals from each ear reaching the brain, so people who are deaf in one ear find it almost impossible to locate the direction of a sound.

Stereo sound systems

Most people enjoy listening to music of some sort. Early radios and hi-fi equipment used a mono system – all the sound came from the same direction, from a single speaker. This gave an artificial feeling, and could not reproduce the sounds as they would have been heard live.

As technology advanced, stereo systems were developed. Sounds were recorded from left and right positions in the concert hall, and fed to left and right speakers. By putting the two speakers at each side of the room, a much more accurate reproduction of the sound could be achieved. Personal stereo sound systems send a different sound directly to each ear via a headphone.

Modern technology is introducing new systems all the time, with quadrophonic sound (four speakers) and more. In the world around us, sounds come from all directions. Surround sound systems, used in cinemas and in many homes, use multiple speakers to create a realistic soundscape.

A dog can locate a sound in one of 32 positions, while a human can only locate it in one of 8 positions.

IN FOCUS: ACCURATE ANIMALS

Many animals are able to locate sounds more accurately than humans. A cat can accurately locate two sounds half a metre apart at a distance of 18 metres (59 feet). A dog is able to pinpoint the direction of a sound very accurately indeed. Imagine a circle divided into 32 equal segments: a dog can locate exactly which segment a sound comes from. A human's hearing is much less accurate; we cannot pinpoint a sound more accurately than to one-eighth of the circle, in other words, four of the dog's segments put together.

Hearing assessment

Hearing is a complex sense, so assessment of a person's hearing requires several different tests. Routine hearing tests can be carried out as part of a general health check by a family doctor, but if a problem is suspected, specialist tests can be carried out by an **audiologist**.

Physical examination

A doctor will examine the ear using an otoscope. This is an instrument that contains a light and a magnifying lens, and allows the doctor to see the ear canal and **eardrum**. During a physical examination, the doctor will check for excess wax, foreign objects, eardrum damage, and signs of infection. This examination may clearly show the cause of any hearing loss, and the doctor can prescribe appropriate treatment. If the doctor can find no reason for a hearing loss, the patient may be referred to an audiologist for specialist tests.

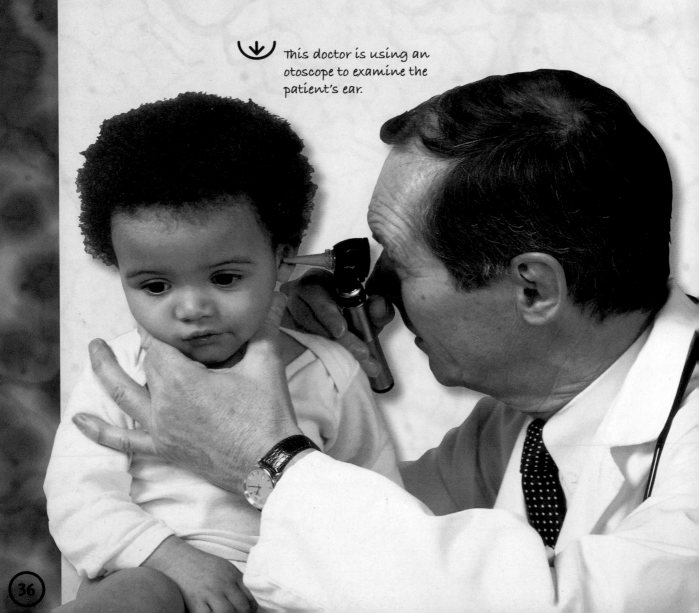

This doctor is using an otoscope to examine the patient's ear.

Specialist assessment

An audiologist will attempt to find the extent and cause of hearing loss. The tests can show the **frequency** range and the levels of intensity of sounds that the patient can hear. Tests can distinguish between problems in the outer ear, **middle ear**, and **inner ear**. The results can be used to suggest appropriate treatment and to ensure that, if a hearing aid is used, it is correctly adjusted to meet the patient's precise needs.

Testing the outer ear

- Pure tone test: this is carried out in a soundproof room, to cut out any background noise. Sounds of different **pitches** and intensities are introduced to the patient via speakers or headphones, and the patient indicates when a sound has been heard. Responses are recorded on a chart called an audiogram.
- Speech audiometry: this estimates the lowest level at which the patient can hear speech.
- Word recognition: this tests how well the patient understands what they hear.

Testing the middle ear

Air pressure is gently increased in the ear canal, and an audiologist measures the movement of the eardrum in response to different sounds. This movement indicates how well the middle ear conducts **sound waves** to the inner ear. The results are shown on a chart called a tympanogram.

Testing the inner ear

The bones of the skull can conduct sounds and can be used to test the inner ear. A special headset is placed on the bone behind the ear, and the patient is asked to respond to sounds that are introduced. The level of hearing is compared with the patient's level of hearing when the same sounds are played via speakers in the room. If the patient hears the sounds at the same level via their ear and via the bone, the hearing problem is within the inner ear, because information is not passed to the brain. If the sound is heard more clearly via the bone than via the ear, it indicates that the inner ear is working properly, and that the problem is with the middle ear failing to conduct sound waves to the inner ear.

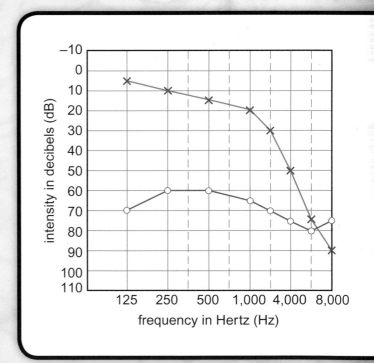

This audiogram shows the hearing of a person with normal hearing in low frequencies but with hearing loss at higher frequencies. The blue line is the left ear, and the red is the right ear.

Deafness

Deafness and hearing loss can affect people of any age. Some people are born deaf and never hear a sound throughout their lives. Some people begin to suffer hearing loss when they are young, while others only become deaf in old age. Whatever the cause and whatever the age, hearing loss and deafness can cause a lot of problems in everyday life.

Causes of hearing loss

Hearing loss can result from many things. The ears may be damaged by repeated exposure to very loud sounds, or by an accident. Infections and other diseases may affect the ears and cause permanent damage. Infection of a mother during pregnancy with, for example, rubella, can lead to her baby's ears being damaged and not developing properly. Some rare types of ear problem are hereditary.

Mild or severe?

Some people suffer only mild hearing loss. They may, for example, find it difficult to hear conversation if there is a lot of background noise, and may need to turn up the volume on the television to hear it clearly. This level of hearing loss requires only minor changes to a person's lifestyle to allow them to carry on as normal.

At the other end of the range are people who can hear absolutely nothing at all. Normal life is very difficult for them, and they often need a lot of help and support to enable them to live independently.

Between these two extremes are many people who have a significant loss of hearing but, with some help, are able to live independent and active lives.

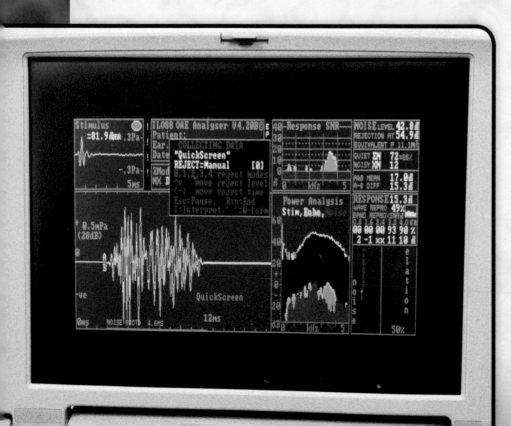

Modern technology can analyse a person's hearing in great detail. The screen in this picture is displaying the results of a test to detect abnormalities in the cochlea.

Restricted frequency range

Some people have a restricted **frequency** range that they can hear. For example, they may be able to hear low, male voices clearly, but struggle to pick up higher, female voices. This restriction may be slight, with only a small, undetectable frequency range that causes few problems. However, if the range of frequencies a person can detect is very narrow, they may experience many problems.

 This child is undergoing a hearing assessment. The sooner the hearing problems are detected and treated, the sooner she can begin to learn and develop her language skills.

The age factor

Hearing plays a very important part in the learning process. As babies, we hear the sound of our mother's voice and learn the familiar patterns of language from her and from other people around us. We become used to everyday sounds and begin to link them with events that happen, for example, when the telephone rings, somebody picks the receiver up and speaks. Without this early learning, understanding everyday life is very difficult. The sooner a child's hearing loss is detected, assessed, and, if possible, treated, the smaller its impact on their learning will be. Adults who lose their hearing have already usually completed their education so, although it may cause difficulties for them, it does not prevent them from achieving their potential.

HEALTH FOCUS: Hearing problems and sport

People with hearing problems can take part in sport (see page 43). Team sports, which rely on reactions to a team member's call, may not be easy. However, many athletic events do not rely on the ability to hear and individual sports, such as golf and swimming, are all possible.

Sign language

We rely on being able to talk to each other. Without this, communication is difficult. Deaf people who cannot hear normal speech can communicate with each other and with people with normal hearing by using sign language.

Developing sign language

Centuries ago, in strict monasteries where monks were not allowed to talk to each other, systems of signs were used for communication. In the 16th century, an Italian doctor explored the possibilities of using a similar system to help deaf people and, in 1620, the first book about teaching a sign language to deaf people was published.

The spread of sign language

In 18th-century Europe, several different systems of sign language developed, each corresponding to the spoken language of a particular country. An American, Thomas Hopkins Gallaudet, travelled to Europe and learned about the methods in use there. He founded the first school for deaf people in the United States. Others took up his ideas, and more schools and colleges for the deaf soon opened, all of which used sign language.

Use of sign language spread, allowing communication between deaf people and those who could hear. Now, in Europe, British Sign Language (BSL) is officially recognized as a minority language. In the United States, qualifications in American Sign Language are even accepted as a second language as part of the entry requirements to many colleges and universities.

Using sign language

Many public meetings and conferences have an interpreter who stands on the stage or platform next to the speakers, in full view of the audience. The interpreter signs the words as they are spoken, allowing deaf people to participate and understand what is being said. News broadcasts on television also often have an interpreter, shown in a box on part of the screen.

 This boy is learning sign language.

IN FOCUS: A SIGN LANGUAGE ALPHABET

Using two hands, you can make the signs that stand for each letter of the alphabet. With these, you can spell out a word or sentence that can be understood by anybody who reads sign language. This method is called "Signed English" (SE).

An alternative approach is that used by American Sign Language (ASL). In this language, signs are used to explain ideas rather than to spell out whole words. This is much quicker than spelling out individual words, conveying the meaning rather than exact sentences. For example, instead of spelling out "I have three dogs" an ASL user would make a sign for three, a sign for dog, and then point to himself, saying "Three dogs, me".

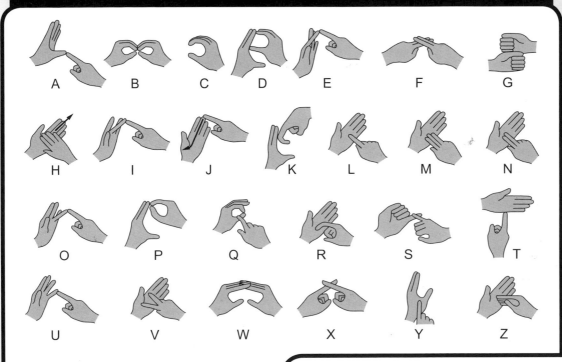

 These diagrams show the signs for each letter of the alphabet. Can you work out how to spell your name, or the town you live in?

Numbers have signs, too. You can use number signs one after another, for example, three followed by five means 35.

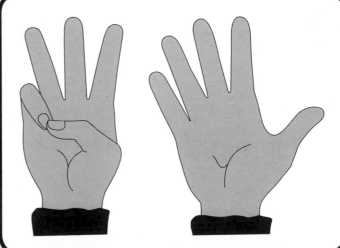

Coping with
deafness

Deafness can make everyday tasks difficult but, with the right help and support, many problems can be overcome. Many devices are now available to help deaf people and, as technology advances, new equipment is constantly being developed.

Communication

Hearing aids are used by many deaf people to help them to hear sounds around them. When we speak, our lips move to make the sounds of words. By watching these movements very carefully, you can work out the sounds that the person is making. This is called "lip reading". With practice, people can become very skilled at understanding speech in this way.

Videophones allow deaf people to communicate with each other. An ordinary telephone line is used, along with a computer or special video camera. When you dial the number and your call is answered, you and the person you have called can see a picture of each other. You can then have a conversation using sign language.

Everyday life

Many things around the home use sound to tell us things. The door bell chimes, the telephone rings, the oven timer bleeps. If you are deaf, all of these things are useless. Instead of sounds, they can be fitted with lights so that a deaf person can see the signal instead of hearing it. Fire and smoke alarms can have special lighting effects so that a deaf person can be alerted to danger.

Hearing dogs can be trained to respond to sounds, and are as important to deaf people as guide dogs are to the blind.

 This man is deaf. He is using adapted telephone equipment to help him to communicate.

Subtitles for television programmes and films allow a deaf person to read a summary of what is being said. These allow them to follow a programme or film in the same way that you can use subtitles to follow a film in a foreign language.

There is no reason why deaf people should not enjoy a social life. Many theatres and concert halls now have a "hearing loop" installed, allowing them to experience the sounds of the performance.

Achieving success

In the past, deaf children were not expected to achieve very much. Today, however, deaf people are proving all the time that being deaf need not prevent anyone from being very successful.

Marlee Matlin is very successful despite being deaf. She is a film star and has won many awards, including an Oscar for Best Actress. She has her own production company and makes television films.

HEALTH FOCUS: Feeling sound

Evelyn Glennie is profoundly deaf but, despite this disability, she has become one of the greatest percussion players of our times. She gives solo performances at concert halls around the world, and her playing is admired and respected by musicians everywhere. Evelyn says that she feels different sounds in different parts of her body.

Here, Miha Zupan is playing basketball for Slovenia in a Euroleague match – being deaf has not stood in the way of his sporting success!

What can go wrong with my ears?

This book has explained the different parts of human ears, why they are important, and how they can be damaged by injury and illness. The table below summarizes some of the problems that can affect people's ears. It also gives information about treating each problem and some of the ways you can prevent ear problems.

Illness or injury	Cause	Symptoms	Prevention	Treatment
cauliflower ear	frequent abrasion and rubbing of the pinna, usually sport-related	lumpy, disfigured pinnae	protect ears by wearing a helmet or taping ears to the side of the head	plastic surgery may be possible for severe cases
ear infections	infection by bacteria or viruses	earache, pain, deafness, ringing noises in ear, possibly pus discharge	good standard of personal hygiene. Healthy diet with plenty of fresh fruit and vegetables to provide vitamins needed for good health.	depends on exact cause, but antibiotics may be used to treat bacterial infections
excess wax	build up of excess wax in ear canal	hearing reduced in affected ear, irritation	good standard of personal hygiene	wax softened with warm oil and then removed by doctor or nurse
stuck objects	object stuck in ear canal	hearing reduced in affected ear	never put anything in your ear! Even cleaning the ear with tissues or cotton buds can cause a problem.	careful removal of object by doctor or nurse
deafness	a number of possible causes, but many are due to prolonged exposure to loud noises leading to damage to the cochlea	gradual deterioration in hearing	keep MP3 players at low volume and avoid long periods of use. Wear protective ear muffs or ear plugs if working in noisy environment (or at a loud concert).	wearing a hearing aid may improve hearing

Many health problems can be avoided by good health behaviour. This is called prevention. Taking regular exercise and getting plenty of rest are important, as is eating a balanced diet. This is important in your teenage years, when your body is still developing.

Remember, if you think something is wrong with your body, you should always talk to a trained medical professional such as a doctor or a school nurse. Regular medical check-ups are an important part of maintaining a healthy body.

Find out more

Books to read

Blood, Bones, and Body Bits (Horrible Science), Nick Arnold (Scholastic, 2008 [new edition]).

Seeing, Hearing, and Smelling the World (Brain Works), Carl Y. Saab (Chelsea House Publishers, 2007)

What Does It Mean To Be Deaf?, Louise Spilsbury (Heinemann Library, 2003)

Websites to visit

www.kidshealth.org/teen/diseases_conditions/sight/hearing_impairment.html
Website designed for young people with information about how ears work, ear health, and hearing problems.

www.bbc.co.uk/humanbody/body/factfiles/hearing/hearing.shtml
Website providing information about hearing, and hearing problems.

http://faculty.washington.edu/chudler/bigear.html
Neuroscience website with detailed information about ears and hearing.

http://www.ci-4teenz.com
Website for young people with information about cochlear implants.

Glossary

abrasion damage caused by repeated rubbing

antibiotics drugs used to fight infections. They destroy micro-organisms, such as bacteria or fungi, but are not effective against viruses.

anvil one of the tiny bones in the middle ear

audiologist person who carries out tests to find out how well people can hear

auditory nerve nerve that carries signals from the ear to the brain

bacteria microbes that can be useful or that can cause disease

basilar membrane membrane that lies beneath the hair cells of the spiral organ

cartilage strong, flexible material that protects bones

cochlea bony spiral in the inner ear

eardrum membrane that forms a partition between the outer ear and the middle ear

eustachian tube tube connecting the middle ear and the nasopharynx

frequency how often a sound happens

genetic to do with passing characteristics from one generation to the next

hair cell cell with tiny hairs sticking out from its surface

hammer one of three ossicles, the tiny bones in the middle ear

inner ear fluid-filled innermost part of the ear

ligament strong cord that binds joints together

membrane thin layer of tissue

middle ear air-filled middle section of the ear

ossicles three tiny bones of the middle ear

otolith granules that cover the surface of the otolithic membrane

otolithic membrane jelly-like membrane that lies on top of the hair cells in the utricle and saccule

oval window membrane that forms a partition between the middle ear and the inner ear

pinna (plural, **pinnae**) flap of skin-covered cartilage that juts out at the side of your head

pitch how high or low a sound is

radial fibres fine threads arranged like the spokes of a wheel

round window small, membrane-covered opening between the middle ear and inner ear, below the oval window

saccule part of the inner ear concerned with balance

semicircular canal one of three ducts in the inner ear that are concerned with balance

sound wave vibrations made by a sound source

spiral organ part of the inner ear that responds to vibrations

stirrup one of the tiny bones in the middle ear

tectorial membrane membrane that lies on top of hair cells in the spiral organ

utricle part of the inner ear concerned with balance

virus microbe that uses the body's own cells to make copies of itself

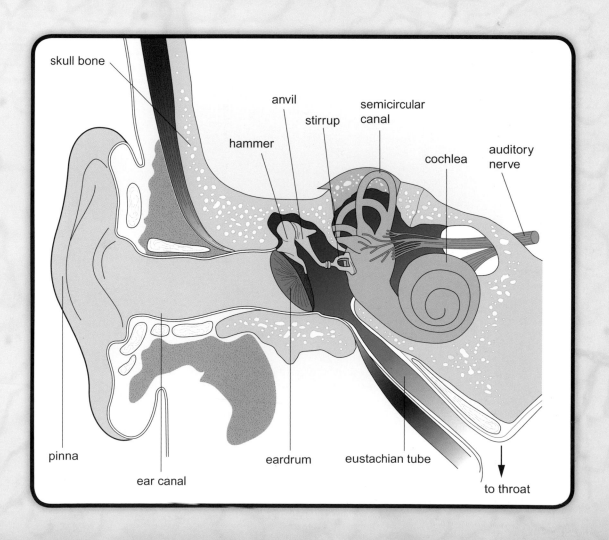

Index

Ears

Injury, Illness, and Health

Revised and updated

Carol Ballard

Heinemann
LIBRARY

www.heinemannlibrary.co.uk
Visit our website to find out more information about Heinemann Library books.

To order:

☎ Phone +44 (0) 1865 888066

🖷 Fax +44 (0) 1865 314091

💻 Visit www.heinemannlibrary.co.uk

Heinemann Library is an imprint of **Capstone Global Library Limited**, a company incorporated in England and Wales having its registered office at 7 Pilgrim Street, London, EC4V 6LB - Registered company number: 6695582

"Heinemann" is a registered trademark of Pearson Education Limited, under licence to Capstone Global Library Limited

Text © Capstone Global Library Limited 2009
First edition published in 2003
The moral rights of the proprietor have been asserted.

Edited by Andrew Farrow, Adrian Vigliano, and Pollyanna Poulter
Designed by Steven Mead and Geoff Ward
Original illustrations © Capstone Global Library Limited 2003
Illustrated by David Woodroffe
Picture research by Ruth Blair
Originated by Heinemann Library
Printed and bound in China by CTPS

ISBN 978 0 431157 47 4 (hardback)
13 12 11 10 09
10 9 8 7 6 5 4 3 2 1

ISBN 978 0 431157 61 0 (paperback)
13 12 11 10 09
10 9 8 7 6 5 4 3 2 1

British Library Cataloguing in Publication Data
Ballard, Carol
Ears. - 2nd ed. - (Body focus)
1. Ear - Juvenile literature 2. Ear - Diseases - Juvenile literature 3. Hearing - Juvenile literature 4. Deafness - Juvenile literature
I. Title
612.8'5
A full catalogue record for this book is available from the British Library.

Acknowledgements
We would like to thank the following for permission to reproduce photographs: Action Plus: p. **11**; Alamy Images: pp. **6**, **36**; AKG London: p. **19**; Corbis: pp. **8** left (Jens Nieth/Zefa), **8** right (Image Source), **20**, **24** (Sergio Pitamitz), **25** (Martyn Goddard); Getty Images: pp. **27** (Photodisc), **42** and **43** (AFP); Photolibrary Group: pp. **18** (BSIP Medical), **39** (Age Fotostock); Popperfoto: p. **23**; Science Photo Library: pp. **7**, **10** (Hattie Young), **13** (CNRI), **14** (Dr. Kari Lounatmaa), **15** (Professor Tony Wright, Institute of Laryngology & Otology), **31** (John Bavosi), **36** (CC Studio), **38** (Annabella Bluesky), **40**.

Cover photograph of the middle and inner ear reproduced with permission of Science Photo Library (Medical rf.com).

We would like to thank David Wright for his invaluable help in the preparation of this book.

Every effort has been made to contact copyright holders of material reproduced in this book. Any omissions will be rectified in subsequent printings if notice is given to the publishers.